To Bev & Scott
" dreamy days in Dorset "
thinking of you
much love Robert

Feb 2002

D1482072

First published in 1999 by Dorset Books
Copyright © 1999 Roger Holman

ISBN 1 871164 70 2

British Library Cataloguing-in-Publication-Data
A CIP data record for this book is available from the British Library

DORSET BOOKS
Official Publisher to Dorset County Council
Halsgrove House
Lower Moor Way
Tiverton EX16 6SS
T: 01884 243242
F: 01884 243325
www.halsgrove.com

Printed and bound in Singapore
by UIC Printing & Packaging Pte Ltd

The River Stour.

CONTENTS

East Dorset's boundary is a line drawn from Sixpenny Handley nearly to Poole. It is an area that has seen the most development of the last few years and this seems set to continue.

This is not so on Cranborne Chase, a vast tract of land spreading across into Wiltshire and taking its name from the village of Cranborne. Today it is an attractive, quiet backwater but once was the centre of one of the largest and most important hunting forests in the country. In the early nineteenth century it had an estimated deer population of between twelve and twenty thousand and everything was made subordinate to its needs. Treves called it a 'rough mysterious country' and it did in fact attract a lawless population of poachers, smugglers, thieves and murderers making it a perfect refuge for those who needed to escape from society. But that all started to change with the 1830 Act of Parliament abolishing hunting rights. Much of the forest was felled and the ground ploughed, destroying the habitat that had sheltered the deer and the lawless for hundreds of years. Now it is open arable country with little to show of what Hardy described as 'One of the few remaining woodlands in England of undoubted primeval date, wherein Druidical mistletoe is still found on aged oaks, and where enormous yew trees, not planted by the hand of man, grew as they had grown when they were pollarded for bows.'

Wimborne's long history can be traced back to prehistoric times and certainly it would have heard the tramp of Vespasian's conquering Second Legion when they made their base camp at Lake Gates just a little to the west of the town.

The best that Treves could say about Wimborne was that it 'was successfully mediocre' and 'it looks best when seen from a distance'.

It certainly looks attractive from across the Stour water meadows but today most people would disagree about it being mediocre. The magnificent Minster church dominates the town with its twin towers and is complemented by many other fine buildings. It is a friendly bustling place, being popular with its numerous visitors

The River Stour continues on its meandering journey flowing under the very old (1170) and extremely attractive eight-arched bridge at White Mill, past Wimborne until it meets up with the Hampshire Avon in Christchurch Harbour. Bad flooding is almost a thing of the past since the River Authority has taken action to reduce the risk with the introduction of barriers and by keeping the river free of vegetation. It supports a large swan population and on one occasion I counted well over fifty gathered on the riverbank near Throop Mill.

Ackling Dyke, one of the most spectacular Roman roads in Britain, seen in winter.

Ackling Dyke in early summer.

Pamphill. A little village overlooking the Stour which is part of the Kingston Lacy estate, now owned by the National Trust.

Pamphill still has its archetypal village shop and Post Office. Sadly, too many others have disappeared, sacrificed on the altar of progress.

Pamphill. Cricket on the village green still played for fun as it has been for generations.

Kingston Lacy House. Bequeathed by Ralph Bankes to the National Trust with many art treasures.

White Mill Bridge, one of the most attractive bridges in Dorset.

Horton Tower built by Humphrey Sturt about 1700 as a lookout to spot deer herds.

17

Knowlton Church. This ruined fourteenth century church stands in the centre of a pagan circle.
It is believed that human sacrifices took place here and some people still find it oppressive.

Sturminster Marshall.

Wimborne Minster, viewed across the Stour meadows in winter.

Wimborne Minster. Part of the church dates back to Norman times.

*The sloping Philosopher's Tower near Wimborne St Giles was built
by the third Earl of Shaftesbury, known as the Philosopher Earl,
presumably so he could sit and contemplate without distraction.*

Holt Forest.

Long Crichel.

The signal box at Moors Valley miniature steam railway.

Cowgrove, a little village on the Stour is part of the Kingston Lacy estate bequeathed by Ralph Bankes to the National Trust.

Cowgrove.

Badbury Rings is an Iron Age hill fort situated at the junction of two Roman roads on the Kingston Lacy estate. The famous avenue of pollarded beech that leads to the Rings (opposite) was planted by French prisoners after the Napoleonic wars. Originally there were over 300 trees on either side. Now many gaps have appeared due to age and storms so the National Trust have planted new trees further back from the road, which one day will provide replacements.

Red poppies, usually only seen popping up on the verges of new motorways, were in a field near Badbury Rings.

Cranborne was once the administrative centre of Cranborne Chase. Today, however, it is an attractive, quiet backwater showing little sign of once being the great hunting ground of England, although some woods do survive.

Cranborne Chase.

Canford Manor, now a public school.

The River Stour. It is seldom possible to walk along the river for any distance without seeing swans.

The Stour on a frosty morning.

PURBECK, WEYMOUTH & PORTLAND

The Purbeck District boundary cuts across Poole Harbour, includes Brownsea Island, extends north to Lytchett Matravers, and circles in a loop back to the coast encompassing a much larger area than most people consider as being Purbeck.

Hardy would have been very familiar with this part of Dorset because he lived at Bockhampton on the edge of the heathland he named Egdon Heath. In his day the heaths stretched almost continuously from there to the shores of Poole Harbour and beyond. He describes it best in *The Return of the Native*, capturing the brooding mystery and the elemental forces of nature.

But to most people Purbeck is best known for its magnificent coast. From the safe white sandy bay backed by sand dunes at Shell Bay to the holiday resorts of Swanage and Portland, there are soaring cliffs, caves, coves, and bays that make it a walkers' paradise and in the early nineteenth century a smugglers' paradise as well. There are some heaths still in existence but most have gone under the plough. Ironically, the army is responsible for maintaining a sizeable portion of the heath for use as a tank training ground and thereby conserving it as heathland.

Weymouth and Portland have their own District Council but it is unlikely that Weymouth would ever have become so well known had George III not visited it frequently and popularised swimming in the sea. He reputedly took the first swim in his birthday suit while a band struck up God Save The King. The buildings along the sea front are a legacy from those times and indicate how prosperous his patronage made the town.

Apart from stone, Portland was famous for its naval base, made possible by the building of the huge breakwater, mainly by local convict labour. Prince Albert laid the foundation stone in 1849 and nearly a quarter of a century later and having cost one million pounds, the Prince of Wales performed the opening ceremony. The convicts remain but the naval base does not so new uses have to be investigated to help bring employment back to the area.

In 1869 the Portlanders petitioned to have the prison closed down but were unsuccessful. So in Edwardian and Victorian times they exploited the situation by hiring out ponies and traps to visitors who came from all over the country to watch the convicts at work. The tourists are still welcome today, not to view the prisoners but to enjoy the walks and the rugged beauty of an island that is not really an island.

Studland Bay. The sand dunes and gently shelving beach make it a favourite spot for sun worshippers. Now owned by the National Trust.

Coastguard cottages at St Alban's Head.

St Oswald's bay from the promontory of Dungy Head. Durdle Door is just visible.
The magnificent coast between here and White Nothe is very popular with walkers.

The ruins of Rufus Castle. Just visible is Pennsylvania Castle, built for the grandson of the founder of Pennsylvania in America.

Poole Harbour, second only to Sydney in the hierarchy of world harbours. It is a paradise for sailors and now a busy commercial port for cross channel ferries.

Poole Harbour.

*Overlooking Swanage and Ballard Down in the Purbecks, with
the Isle of Wight in the distance, on an unusually clear day.*

Isle of Purbeck.

Agglestone Rock on the Purbeck Heath is such a prominent and unusual landmark that it has inevitably generated much folklore. The best known is that the Devil was responsible for hurling the rock from the Isle of Wight but it fell short of his target Corfe Castle.

Joggers on Purbeck Heath on a frosty morning.

Looking across to Brownsea from Godlingston Heath.

Corfe village.

Corfe Castle stands on a natural steep-sided hillock guarding the only break in the 12-mile stretch of the Purbeck Hills.
Even in ruins it is stunningly photogenic and seems to have grown out of the hill rather than been built upon it. Treves described
the little stone village as 'a wrinkled little place in the winter of its age, lying at the foot of its castle like a faithful hound.'

Upwey has a superb setting in a steep-sided valley close to Weymouth.

The walk up to Swyre Head. A marvellous place to view the coast in both directions.

Tyneham village is just a ruin but it is possible even now to visualise what an idyllic place it must have been, snuggling in a valley close to Worbarrow Bay. Taken over by the Army during the Second World War but never returned to the villagers, it is part of a sad story of broken promises.

Creech in the Purbecks is a lovely valley sheltered from the sea by a second ridge of hills and beautiful in all seasons with many deciduous trees.

Steeple, Isle of Purbeck overlooked by the great whaleback of Smedmore Hill.

The Tout completes the southern side of Worbarrow Bay. It is within the military firing range so only accessible at certain times but well worth the walk from Tyneham.

Until the fourteenth century Wareham, on the River Frome, was a thriving port but it's importance declined due to the silting of the river and the advent of larger ships.

River Frome.

Chesil Beach, a phenomenon that is not repeated anywhere else in the world.
It is a treacherous coast for mariners. Hardy named it Dead Man's Bay.

Lulworth Cove. One of the most popular places on the coast.

65

Windspit is a great place to watch the waves break over the rocks on a stormy day.

WEST DORSET

West Dorset lies west of a line stretching roughly from Sherborne down to the coast and including Dorchester, but excluding Weymouth and Portland. Although there has been some development around the larger towns, such as Prince Charles' high profile project at Poundbury near Dorchester, which incidentally I find particularly attractive, this area has changed very little over the centuries.

A small village viewed from a nearby hill, stone cottages, often thatched and clustered protectively around the village church is typical and what many people think of as true Dorset.

Most roads are narrow with high hedges and some have grass growing down the centres. In summertime the roadside verges and banks are a picture, overflowing with a great variety of wild flowers, nature's own garden. Monica Hutchings, in her book *Inside Dorset* remembered a day's picnic on the downs, when she picked a bouquet of over fifty varieties.

Ralph Wightman wrote 'This is a wholly delightful land and even the lack of signposts is no serious drawback. Every lane leads to a pleasant spot even if it is not one you are seeking'. Although written over fifty years ago, this could still be said today.

Near the western boundary and in sight of Devon is Pilsdon Pen, at 910 feet, the highest hill in Dorset and sporting a bare top, capped by an ancient hill fort. Nearby is its partner, Lewesdon Hill, slightly lower and markedly different with a thickly wooded summit. The old local saying 'as alike as Lewesdon and Pilsdon' means not alike at all, just a nice example of rural irony. Both overlook the Marshwood Vale, a basin of blue impervious clay, which is surrounded by hills making it feel quite cut off and isolated.

The coast from Lyme to Weymouth proudly claims the highest sea cliff on the South Coast at Golden Cap and unique Chesil Beach, a twelve-mile stretch of graded pebbles protecting the largest inland lagoon in Britain. It is not only the habitat for a great deal of marine life but also the swans of the famous Abbotsbury Swannery.

Passing through the unprepossessing little village of Tolpuddle, it is hard to believe the events that occurred here in 1831 were eventually to bring about so much social change. Forever, Tolpuddle will be associated with the Martyrs and the first flickering of Trade Unionism.

Justice was harsh in those days but even harsher in Judge Jeffreys' time: the Hanging Judge presided over the Bloody Assizes in Dorchester, condemning many men to be hanged drawn and quartered, including some supporters of the Duke of Monmouth after their landing at Lyme and his ill-fated attempt to claim the throne of England.

St Catherine's Chapel, Abbotsbury. Built in the fourteenth century it is seen here from the coast road.

69

Abbotsbury from the West.

A profusion of flowers on a roadside bank.

Bridport with the distinctive Colmer's Hill in the distance. Some 700 years ago a rope making industry was established here with the most prosperous period being in the eighteenth and early nineteenth centuries. The old saying 'Stabbed by the Bridport Dagger' means being hanged. Bridport rope had many uses!

Beaminster sits in an amphitheatre surrounded by green rolling hills.

From Quarry Hill looking West toward Chideock Manor.

Looking toward Bradpole from Quarry Hill reveals how the ground rises in knolls and gives the landscape a special character.

Came House, Winterborne Came. The rectory, just visible on the left, was where
William Barnes, the Dorset poet, was rector from 1862 until his death.

The rolling countryside west of Dorchester, looking north off the old Roman road.

Batcombe, situated under the great wall of Batcombe Ridge, has wonderful views across West Dorset.
It was famous as the centre of the Dorset Blue Vinney cheese industry but alas no longer.

Eggardon provides the best views of any hill fort in Dorset. To the west is Golden Cap and across the Marshwood Vale to Pilsdon Pen. Even the chalk cliffs of Beer in Devon can be seen on a clear day.

The Blackmore Vale overlooking Buckland Newton after a light dusting of snow has caught the hilltops.

Minterne Magna.

Minterne Magna, home of the Digby family.

Cerne Abbas.

The Abbot's Hall Porch is all that remains of the Abbey but it does give a hint of what a beautiful building it must have been until Henry VIII decided otherwise.

Cerne Abbas village itself has some very attractive old buildings
but it is the Cerne Giant which creates the most interest.

Sherborne New Castle, built by Sir Walter Raleigh on the site of a much smaller building. It was purchased by the Digbys shortly after Raleigh's execution.

Sherborne Old Castle was also owned by Raleigh but, after trying unsuccessfully to renovate it, he decided to build himself a new one nearby.

This is the seat where Raleigh liked to sit watching what was the main road between Sherborne and Dorchester. Whilst here having a quiet smoke, his servant reputedly came along, thought he was on fire and tipped a bowl of water over him.

Sherborne Abbey, considered by some to be the most important piece of architecture in Dorset.

St John's Almshouses, Sherborne.

Maiden Castle, a massive Iron Age hill fort near Dorchester.

Overlooking Dorchester from Maiden Castle.

93

Nether Cerne is a small but beautiful hamlet consisting
of a church, a farm and a few other buildings.

Portesham was the home of the other Hardy, Nelson's 'kiss me Hardy', seen here from the Abbotsbury Plains with White Nothe in the distance.

Early Summer near Winterborne Zelston.

Cony's Castle is an Iron Age hill fort situated near the Devon border.

*An ancient oak growing on Powerstock Common, one of
many sites owned by the Dorset Wildlife Trust.*

Lillington, a small village near Sherborne with cottages clustered around the church.

Evershot and Tess cottage. Little changed from Hardy's day.

Lewesdon from Pilsdon Pen.

Colmer's Hill is a very prominent landmark usually seen against the sky, but photographed here from the adjacent Quarry Hill. The Dorset Craft Guild based their logo on the outline of the hill and trees.

Near Dolls Ash, the bare upland farm Hardy called Flintcombe Ash where Tess laboured in the great swede fields. 'A hundred odd acres in one patch without a tree in sight'.

From Golden Cap, the highest sea cliff on the South Coast looking North West.

105

Steep hills run both in and out of Chideock and it is the last remaining village of any size that still has to suffer the relentless pounding of the A35 traffic.

From the outskirts of Dorchester looking east.

Melbury Bubb, a tiny village sheltering under Bubb Down Hill.

The view from Pilsdon Pen across the Marshwood Vale.

West Milton is a little village set in some of the best West Dorset countryside.
It was home to Kenneth Allsop, the well-known broadcaster.

North Porton near Powerstock.

*Up Cerne is a tiny hamlet in a lovely setting off
the main Dorchester to Sherborne road.*

St Catherine's Chapel above Abbotsbury with Portland in the distance.

Fishing on the river near Frampton.

114

Water crowfoot in flower on the River Frome at Muckleford.

Linseed fields near Bere Regis.

NORTH DORSET

North Dorset is bordered by Wiltshire in the North and Purbeck in the South. It is similar in many ways to West Dorset although the countryside is more open and the villages more scattered. The Blackmore Vale, occupies the western part and as in Hardy's day, agriculture still plays a dominant role. The ancient hedgerows have not been ripped out which has meant the landscape has kept an intimate scale with tiny fields and winding lanes. One of the best places to view the Vale and indeed a large part of the county is from Bulbarrow—the second highest hill in Dorset. The vistas are stunning, disappearing in a blue grey mist. It is said that on a fine day seven counties can be seen from the summit.

Shaftesbury, one of the oldest and highest towns in England, provides another good place to view the Blackmore Vale. Its character is largely unspoilt with many visitors searching out Gold Hill, a romantic steep cobbled street made immortal by the Hovis advertisements.

The Stour, Dorset's main river, meanders quietly through the Stour valley passing Sturminster Newton, looping around Hod Hill and travelling on through Blandford, ensuring the land is very fertile because of the silt brought down by flooding since time immemorial. Our ancestors made good use of the free power that the river provided by building many mills serving the community with food and work. I never cease to wonder at the difficulties involved in the construction of these mills with their accompanying locks and millponds, all without the benefit of today's machinery. Sturminster Newton Mill is one that has been renovated and can now be viewed at certain times.

The village of Marnhull is of Saxon origin and was a site where Iron Age people once lived. Hardy called it Marlott and used it for the setting of some of the action of his best-loved novel, *Tess of the d'Urbervilles*. It is where her cottage and The Pure Drop Inn are situated.

High on the hill overlooking Fontmell Down is the privately owned airfield of Compton Abbas. It is quite small with a grass runway but very popular with weekend fliers. The wartime airfield at Tarrant Rushton has been returned to agriculture. All that remains is a hangar and a memorial to the Glider and Airborne troops. This was the last piece of England that many of those brave men stepped upon before making their supreme sacrifice at Arnhem.

Compton Abbas has many thatched cottages sheltering in a lovely setting under Melbury Hill.

Compton Down after an unusually heavy fall of snow.

Melbury Hill in snow.

Melbury Hill from the top of Zig-Zag Hill.

Path to Ringmoor where the National Trust owns 134 acres.
From here there are stunning views across the Blackmoor Vale.

Norton Wood near Durweston in springtime.

From the base of Hod Hill looking across the Stour Valley.

Hod Hill early morning.

Fontmell Down Nature Reserve, managed by the Dorset Wildlife Trust.

Hilton.

Milton Abbey and school…

130

...set deep in a valley amongst the chalk hills.

Iwerne Minster, one of the few churches in Dorset possessing a stone steeple.

Marnhull, Hardy's Marlott in Tess of the d'Urbervilles.

Hinton St Mary Mill on the Stour.

A peaceful scene as the sun sets.

Fiddleford Manor and Mill. Parts of the Manor date back to the 1370s. Now looked after by English Heritage.

Fiddleford.

River Stour at Shillingstone, in flood.

The River Stour in winter, at Sturminster Newton.

Sturminster Newton Mill.

141

*Duncliff Hill is actually two hills west of Shaftesbury and now
a nature reserve. It overlooks Blackmore Vale.*

*Gold Hill, Shaftesbury must rank with Corfe Castle
as one of the most photographed places in Dorset.*

On the Dorset border near Shaftesbury, looking into Wiltshire.